BOSCH~BRUEGEL

AND THE NORTHERN RENAISSANCE

By CLAUDIA LYN CAHAN
and CATHERINE RILEY

AVENEL BOOKS

NEW YORK

Bosch Bruegel and the Northern Renaissance
© MCMLXXX by Fabbri Editori, Milan, Italy
All Rights Reserved
First U.S. Edition published 1980 by Avenel Books
distributed by Crown Publishers Inc.
Printed in Italy by Fabbri Editori, Milan.
a   b   c   d   e   f   g   h   i

Library of Congress Cataloging in Publication Data
Cahan, Claudia Lyn.
Bosch, Bruegel, and the Northern Renaissance.
1. Bosch, Hieronymus van Aken, known as, d. 1516.
2. Painting, Renaissance—Germany.
3. Bruegel, Pieter, the elder, d. 1569. 4. Painting, Renaissance
—Belgium—Flanders. 5. Allegories. 6. Symbolism in
art. I. Riley, Catherine, joint author. II. Title.
ND653.B65C33 1979 759.03 79-21697
ISBN 0-517-30373-6

The conquest of the visible world, the exploration and the introduction of a new sense of realism

During the 150 years from the end of the fourteenth century to the middle of the sixteenth century, the European world view changed irrevocably. This period, which saw the waning of the Middle Ages, the Renaissance, and the Reformation, gave men a new concept of themselves, in which they and their physical universe replaced purely spiritual concerns as a prime object of attention and study. This was reflected in the new perspectives, forms, and techniques of their art. Each country in Europe expressed the change in its own way: in the south, in Italy, the artistic revolution was more fundamental, an abrupt break with the traditions of the past; but in the north, in Flanders, those traditions were used as a point of departure.

However, in both areas, the goal was the same – the attempt to conquer the visible world, to explore and to bring to art a new sense of realism.

The work of Jan van Eyck, Rogier van der Weyden, Petrus Christus, Hugo van der Goes, Hans Memling, Hieronymus Bosch, and Pieter Bruegel the Elder spans this time of change, and each of these painters played a role in the evolution of the Northern Renaissance. Though firmly rooted in their native region, the Flemish masters, through their portrayal of intense realism, had an impact that extended far beyond their own country and their own time.

During the Middle Ages, painting had played a relatively minor role to that of architecture and sculpture, existing mainly as a decorative art in the service of religious ideals and institutions. However, by the fifteenth century, Christian philosophy began to change its position on the nature of the world. The growing ideas that the godhead was implicit in every element of nature created the possibility for the world and its beauty to serve as a source of religious inspiration. With the dawning Renaissance, rigid concepts of the world that had been held for more than a thousand years began to give way to a growing curiosity and an exciting rediscovery of the physical universe. Nature and man were suddenly worthy of an attention and an investigation they had not been given since antiquity.

These ideals, spurred by a nominalist philosophy that turned men from the study of universals to the search for the individual, led the artist to develop techniques he could use to reproduce accurately the breadth of the life he began to see around him. This investigation and reproduction of nature had its beginnings in the International Gothic Style of painting, the leading form of which was found in the north in miniatures. In the early years of the fifteenth century, a group of Flemings who had settled in France, the Limbourg Brothers, produced the wellknown *Book of Hours of the Duc de Berry*. There, on the calendar pages, they painted, in intimate detail, the lives of peasants and noblemen as they experienced the passing seasons. In these tiny paintings, there are light and shadow, distant landscapes, and minute but perfect flowers, birds, and beasts. It was left to the painters of the Northern Renaissance to develop these ideals and bring them to full-sized painting.

Jan van Eyck

The first artist to fully realize the ideals of fifteenth century Flemish realism was Jan van Eyck (1390-1441). He is closely associated with the town of Bruges, a great trading center of late medieval Flanders that has been called the birthplace of Flemish painting. Van Eyck spent a good portion of his life as a court painter, serving John of Bavaria from 1422 to 1424 and moving a year later to the court of Philip the Good, Duke of Burgundy, who was a great patron of the arts and was building a new palace in Bruges. Their relationship was one of mutual respect and admiration, and van Eyck made several secret journeys on business for the duke. Van Eyck also worked for wealthy Italians who resided in Bruges – most notably Giovanni Arnolfini – and through them, his fame spread to Italy.

For centuries, the debate raged as to whether van Eyck was the inventor of oil paints. It has generally been conceded that he was not – as, indeed, no single individual was – but his method of using oils did enhance their development and perpetuation. Van Eyck experimented by mixing his colors with various oils and varnishes to obtain a medium that was fluid enough to enable

paramount example of this mixture of symbols and pragmatic detail. Upon close examination, we see that every fine grain in the wooden floor is included. The weave of the fabrics – a favorite subject of painters whose patrons were often involved in the cloth trade – is recreated. Every hair in the fur trim of Giovanni Arnolfini's coat is taken into account. The painting is also full of inscriptions and symbols. The stations of the cross are painted on the frame of the mirror hanging behind the couple, while in the mirror is reflected the images of the painter and a possible witness to the wedding. The dog is a symbol of filial devotion, and the fruit on the windowsill represents propagation. Van Eyck's contemporaries easily understood such symbols, and they derived pleasure from deciphering a painting.

Van Eyck gave equal importance to the purely realistic features and to the symbolic elements of his paintings. In fact, it has been suggested that the former may have been of greater importance here since the painting possibly served as a legal document, a kind of visual marriage license. Perhaps this explains why the artist has placed his signature prominently on the wall above the mirror.

Rogier van der Weyden

Rogier van der Weyden (1399/1400-1464) was the next most influential figure in the development of fifteenth century Flemish painting, and his teacher, the Master of Flemalle, Robert Campin, is considered the third most important leader. Robert Campin did indeed pave the way, but the art of his pupil, van der Weyden, had a more direct impact on Flemish and European painting. Van der Weyden was born in Tournai but lived and worked in Brussels. His excellent command of graphic detail enabled him to use it as a means of dramatic characterization in paintings where the action of the figures is of as great importance as the realistic detail. It has been said that van der Weyden took the lessons he learned from the founders of Flemish realism – that is, from van Eyck and Campin – and blended them into a powerful unity, which was then transmitted to his followers and to the rest of Europe.

him to apply the paint layer by layer, thereby achieving the subtlest effects of light and detail and allowing the darker tones underneath to show through and impart depth and substance to the images. Van Eyck used the very refined and clear oils just then becoming available in the merchant cities of Flanders and mixed them with the new sources of colors arriving on the spice ships from Africa and the East – an innovation that in part accounts for the theory that he discovered oil painting.

His extraordinary use of oil and color was only one aspect of his immense influence. The other was his great desire and ability to perfectly portray reality. No artist had ever been more preoccupied with the presentation of detail, with exactitude of even the finest particle of the natural world. The human eye could take in only a limited perception of reality, but van Eyck went beyond those limits and, with infinite patience, strove to reconstruct, rather than merely represent or suggest reality. It was through his building up of minute details that he realized a complete expression of the whole.

The Arnolfini Wedding (Plates XXVIII and XXIX) is a

Portrait of a Noble Woman -
Washington, National Gallery of Art (Mellon Collection)

A major problem for art historians who wish to study his works is that none of van der Weyden's paintings are known authentically to have been signed by him, and his influence was so great that he had many imitators. Therefore, there are constant controversies as to which pictures can definitely be attributed to him. Van der Weyden achieved great fame, and his works, which were full of warm color and emotion, were well received among his contemporaries. His most crucial contribution to the future of painting was as an intermediary between the Flemish and the Italian art worlds. In 1450, he visited Rome and Florence. The relationship between the Italian and Flemish schools of this time was somewhat one-sided. While the Flemings remained relatively unresponsive to the art of the early Italian Renaissance, the Italians admired the Flemish use of light and color and the prevalence in their paintings of naturalistic details. As a result, after van der Weyden's trip, the Italians developed a more extensive use of landscape and its details, and they began to use contemporary interior settings as the context for religious events. There was also an increased interest in naturalistic lighting and in the textures that different lights created, but, most importantly, through the Flemish, the methods of oil painting reached Southern Europe. The classical, humanist vision and the quasi-scientific preoccupation with perspective of the Italians held much less interest for the Flemish, and it was not until the sixteenth century that they began to be strongly influenced by the Italians.

Petrus Christus

Van der Weyden's influence was evident in the works of Petrus Christus, who flourished in Bruges in the mid-fifteenth century. In all likelihood, he served as an apprentice in van Eyck's shop there, and he was considered the most important master in the city after van Eyck's death. There are aspects of van Eyck's naturalistic and objective tradition in Christus's work. At the same time, Christus's art reflects the teachings of the Master of Flemalle as they were finally expressed in the emotional style of Rogier van der Weyden. Christus's own style was rather heavy, and his best

Portrait of a Woman

Hans Memling

Hans Memling (1440-1494) may have been a pupil of Rogier van der Weyden, because the influence of the older painter is very apparent in his work. Memling was born in Germany and probably received his earliest training there. Yet in style and spirit he was totally Flemish. In 1465, he became a citizen of Bruges, and, in 1467, he was accepted into the painter's guild of that city. He was a very successful artist who enjoyed the admiration of his contemporaries and the patronage of Germans, English, and Spanish. The Medicis and Tommaso Portinari were among the wealthy foreigners who supported his art. A great many of Memling's paintings deal with religious themes, but he also painted many fine portraits, some of the best of which were incorporated in the religious works. He usually worked on large panels, although he was like a miniaturist in his attention to detail. It has been said by many art historians that there is no chronological development or artistic improvement in his works, but a good deal of this criticism may be due to the fact that he was not an innovator but a polisher of the tradition that, by his time, was well established. To twentieth-century eyes, his paintings sometimes appear overly sentimental and almost maudlin, but in the fifteenth century, his gentle rendering of biblical legends, his realistic yet polite portraits, and his famous, almost luminous Madonnas brought him great popularity. His use of sparkling color and his ability to represent light as if it were coming from a single source gave his works a romantic quality that greatly appealed to the merchant princes who were his contemporaries. However, in spite of the international reputation he enjoyed in his own day, he had little effect on the generations who came after him. Not until he was rediscovered by the Romantics of the nineteenth century was his painting again admired and his influence felt.

Hugo van der Goes

Hugo van der Goes (1440-1482) was probably born in Ghent, and

works by far are his portraits. The serenity and simplicity of *Portrait of Edward Grymestone* (Plate XVIII) is characteristic of these paintings. His major contribution in the history of Flemish painting was his practical application of the theories and rules of perspective, which were then being developed by the Italians.

Sitting Young Woman - Montreal, Randall Collection

Sitting Young Woman - Montreal, Randall Collection

Man-tree in a Landscape - Vienna, Albertina Academy

he was active there, becoming a master of the artists' guild in 1467 and dean of the guild from 1473 to 1475. He combined both formal and thematic Italian and Flemish elements in his works. His best known painting is the large triptych, *The Portinari Altarpiece* with *The Adoration of the Shepherds* (Plate XXXIV) as its central panel. It was commissioned by Tommaso Portinari, a wealthy Florentine banker and shipowner who represented the Medici firm in Bruges. The rustic types portrayed in *The Adoration of the Shepherds* point to van der Goes's interest in painting common people. The variety of expressions and the individualistic facial features of the shepherds reflect his fascination for conveying the character of people as seen in their faces. This painting had little influence in van der Goes's own

country since it was almost immediately sent to Florence. However, once there, it had great impact on several Florentine artists.

In 1475, van der Goes entered the Monastery Roode Kloster, located near Brussels. Six years later, he experienced a period of tremendous mental anguish the antecedent of which may in part account for his seeming preoccupation with the emotional makeup of his subjects. In 1481, he collapsed while on a trip to Cologne, and, although his depression and suicidal tendencies became less critical, he died the year after this crisis. He left behind, in his paintings, a unique sense of popular realism, technical advancements in the use of oils, a rich sense of color, and an innovative fantastic landscape.

Hieronymus Bosch

Hieronymus Bosch (1450-1516) was probably born in and derived his name from Hertogenbosch, located in southern Holland near the present Belgian border. Most masters of Bruges, Ghent, Louvain, Haarlem, and Delft – the major centers of Flemish art – were continuing in the traditions established at the beginning of the century by the Master of Flemalle and Jan van Eyck. Hieronymus Bosch departed from these principles and developed from old traditions new forms that expressed his view of the world.

His painting has been called the Gothic twilight, and, of all Flemish art, it best represents some aspects of the waning of the Middle Ages, when witchcraft and plague were rife and there was constant anticipation of an imminent end to the world. While many of the Flemish painted with the pleasure of new world expectations, based on the rise of scientific reasoning, Bosch used many of the new techniques to hark back to the terrors of an earlier age. He described the world as an optical illusion, enticing man with beauty, only to entrap him in temptation. For him, God was not implicit in nature, but Satan surely was. It was for these reasons that Bosch abandoned the purely objective perspectives and descriptive styles of his immediate predecessors. His reality was not of the eye, but of the fevered imagination and deep levels of symbolism of the Late Middle Ages.

There is no historical information concerning Bosch's development as an artist. His teacher is unknown, and he left relatively few works, none of which are dated. His technique was subservient to his greater purpose – warning his fellow man away from the path of sin and indulgence. He did not paint from nature, but when he so desired, he could accurately reproduce details of birds and animals. *The Seven Deadly Sins* (PLate IV) shows how the ideas of realism did have an effect on his medieval sensibilities, even though he did not prescribe to realism's philosophy. He used scenes of everyday life to depict the sins, because it was in daily happenings that the presence of evil took on meaning. It was common at the time to use allegorical figures to represent sin, but each scene painted around the all-seeing eye of God, with an image of Christ at its center, shows contemporary figures. Underneath are the words which warn, "Beware, the Lord sees."

His pessimistic view of life can be seen in *The Haywain* (Plate VI), where the vanity, desire, and greed of the world of men is criticized. He saw the universe as devoid of meaning and man as a puppet of his foolish desires, which lead only to suffering. This thread of pessimism runs through all his work. His monsters and his visual fantasy of the grotesque were personifications of the wickedness he felt existed in the world. Some of his horrific images were inspired by the monsters and beasts in carvings on church pews, in bestiaries, and in illuminated manuscripts, and they carried a very specific symbolism that was immediately apparent to the contemporary viewer.

He was well known until the end of the seventeenth century, and was then forgotten until the end of the nineteenth century. His strongest impact was felt in the art of surrealism. His horrific and fantastic dream images, his sense of the bizarre, as seen especially in *The Garden of Delights* (Plates XIV-XV) had moralistic aims, but his visual rendition of fantasy was the major reason for the surrealist's admiration of Bosch. The alchemical man from *The Garden of Delights* (Plate XVI), with the distorted body and legs in the form of a hollow tree, is truly a nightmarish vision that has its greatest echoes in the art of this century.

Pieter Bruegel the Elder

Pieter Bruegel the Elder (1525/30-1569) did much of his early work in the manner of Bosch. He was nicknamed by his contemporaries "Pieter the Droll," as he, too, had a fondness for the satirical, spookish, and moralizing in art. *The Fall of the Rebel Angels* (Plate XLIX) is directly inspired by Bosch. The fallen angels are transformed into the most incredible monsters, some of whom seem lifted directly from one of Bosch's Hells. However, Bruegel's works seem more purely fanciful rather than full of allusions to medieval mysticism that were so important to

Bosch.

Bruegel's birth connects him to the later Renaissance, but his passion for detail and his late medieval view of the world belong to the fifteenth century. He did travel to France and also to Italy, but neither country's art had much of an influence on his early work. In Italy, he was more impressed with the landscape of the country and the natural beauty of the Alps than he was with the works of the Italian masters. He returned to Antwerp with sketches done of the outdoors. He hadn't even bothered to copy any paintings.

The general consensus of opinion is that Bruegel was born in Breda around 1525 and was probably apprenticed to Pieter Coeck

van Aelst. He originally settled in Antwerp, where he painted almost exclusively for friends and collectors. His reputation in his own time was based on the engravings he did of landscapes and allegorical and religious subjects. His contemporaries judged his work on the basis of its accurate detail and diverse subject matter. In this he excelled, sometimes to the detriment of the overall composition. Early works like *The Fight between Carnival and Lent* (Plate XLVII) and *Children's Games* (Plates L and LI) have a maplike quality, as if he were attempting to describe all of reality as he saw it around him.

In 1563, Bruegel married the daughter of his old master and went to live in Brussels, where he continued to paint until his death in 1569, when he was probably still only in his mid-forties. In his last years, after the move to Brussels, he finally began to be influenced by Italian Renaissance art. His late works, such as the *Peasant Wedding* (Plate LIX) and the *Peasant Dance* (Plates LX and LXI), show this influence in the larger scale of the figures who have been moved closer to the spectator. However, Bruegel remained indifferent to the concept of idealized beauty that was gaining popularity in sixteenth century Flanders.

Despite his innovation in subject matter and his interest in accuracy and realism, Bruegel has been called, by some, the last painter of the Middle Ages. Even his fine landscape series *Months* (Plates LIV, LV, and LXII) seems to have had its source in the miniatures of the medieval calendar books. On the other hand, his faithful portrayal of peasant life led others to term him the first great genre painter, and it is particularly this aspect of his work that had such strong effect on future generations of painters throughout Europe.

Together, the Flemish painters of the fifteenth and sixteenth centuries took the art of painting, in the north, from its medieval subservience to architecture and sculpture and elevated it to a position where it was recognized as man's principal means of artistic expression, throughout Europe during the Renaissance. And, in the process, they established traditions that in later generations would produce such great and varied artists as Rubens, Rembrandt, and van Gogh.

Index of the illustrations

12

XVI - HIERONYMUS BOSCH: The Garden of Delights, detail of Plate XV - *The tree-man is the central monster in this musical Hell. He is alchemical man. His head is thought to be a self-portrait of the artist. The huge ears pierced by an arrow and sliced through by the knife symbolize deafness to the word of God.*

XVII - HIERONYMUS BOSCH: The Garden of Delights, detail of Plate XIV - *Here, both sexes indulge in total sensual pleasures in a world that is abundant and fruitful. There was one theory that Bosch was the member of a heretical sect and painted* The Garden of Delights *as a celebration of its orgiastic rituals. To those who were versed in the complex symbology of the Middle Ages, the work was a clear interpretation of the Last Judgment.*

XVIII - PETRUS CHRISTUS: Portrait of Edward Grymestone - National Gallery, London - *The best works of Christus are his portraits. The beamed ceiling demonstrates his keen understanding of theory and application of the new methods of portraying perspective. The sensitivity of the face reflects the fine introspective treatment for which this painter is noted.*

XIX - PETRUS CHRISTUS: Portrait of a Young Girl - Staatlich Museum, Berlin - *Even though this painting is in a poor state of preservation, it is clear that it had the rare quality of a realistic portrait. Here, Christus demonstrated his interest in the detail and texture of costume at the same time that he caught the individuality of the sitter.*

XX - PETRUS CHRISTUS: Dionysius, the Carthusian - Metropolitan Museum of Art, New York - *This portrait, by Christus, of a Carthusian monk depicted as a saint is painted on a small panel measuring only 8¹/2 by 11⁵/8 inches. Note the fly on the bottom edge, a detail reflecting the naturalistic and objectivist tradition of van Eyck.*

XXI - PETRUS CHRISTUS: Portrait of a Young Man - National Portrait Gallery, London - *It has been said of Christus that coming on the scene of Flemish art, as he did, after van Eyck and van der Weyden, the only way he could express his originality was to turn from the new forms. To some extent he did this, but he could not hide his fascination with texture, light, and detail that is everywhere evident in this painting.*

XXII - ROGIER VAN DER WEYDEN: The Adoration of the Magi - Alte Pinakothek, Munich - *This painting is part of a triptych known as the S. Columba Altarpiece. The other two panels are* The Annunciation *and* The Presentation. *This painting, which is a particularly fine example of van der Weyden's interest in the significance of actions, greatly influenced the painting of Memling (Plates XLII and XLIII).*

XXIII - The Adoration of the Magi, detail of Plate XXII - *Van der Weyden possessed the Flemish command for painting graphic detail. Here, he paints three different degrees of light: the broad daylight in the background, the dark shelter of the hut, and the half-shadows of the awning over the arches. In the background, he has painted a Flemish town with exact detail.*

XXIV - Magdalene - Louvre, Paris - *Van der Weyden's emotional nature was well suited to the portrayal of the Magdalene's repentance. The tears in her eyes are affecting without being sentimental. At the same time, the delight the artist took in portraying the fine textures of her gown and the filmy gauze of her headdress adds a poignant reality to her sorrow.*

XXV - ROGIER VAN DER WEYDEN: Portrait of a Lady - Staatliche Museum, Berlin - *Van Eyck's influence can be seen in this portrait when one compares it to Plate XXX. It is also interesting to compare this painting to Plate XXIV, for van der Weyden has taken equal care with the subdued colors and textures, and the unidealized facial expression suggests the presence of even stronger emotions.*

XXVI - ROGIER VAN DER WEYDEN: The Beheading of St. John - Staatliche Museum, Berlin - *This painting is from the triptych titled* Scenes from the Life of St. John the Baptist. *In the foreground, Salome receives the head of St. John from the executioner. Our eyes travel through several arches to an inner compartment, where the kneeling Salome offers St. John's head to Herod and Herodias at the table.*

XXVII - The Annunciation - c. 1452 - Louvre, Paris - *Part of the famous Braque Triptych, this painting displays all the characteristics of color, technique, and feeling for which van der Weyden became famous throughout Europe. The practice of placing religious scenes within secular settings originated with the Flemish, and the Italian painters of the Renaissance adopted this style from them.*

XXVIII-XXIX - JAN VAN EICK: The Arnolfini Wedding - 1434 - National Gallery, London - *The artist's signature and the date are painted on the wall over the mirror. The painting is a masterpiece in every minute detail, from the little brush by the bed to the slippers on the floor. The wedding couple is surrounded by symbols of marital bliss. The dog, for example, is a symbol of fidelity, and the fruit indicates the hope of fertility.*

XXX - JAN VAN EYCK: Margaretha van Eyck - 1439 - Bruges Museum, Bruges - *This portrait of van Eyck's wife is one of the first where the sitter's eyes look out of the picture at the spectator. Van Eyck married Margaretha in 1434, and later that year they had their first son.*

XXXI - JAN VAN EYCK: The Man with the Red Turban - 1433 - National Gallery, London - *The subject of this painting is debatable. It may be van Eyck's father-in-law or it may be a self-portrait of the artist. Some critics say it is a wealthy merchant about sixty-five years old. It is the finely executed wrinkles around the eyes that lead to the belief in the age of the model.*

XXXII - JAN VAN EYCK: The Adoration of the Lamb - 1432 - St. Bavo, Ghent - *This is the central panel from the base of the Ghent Altarpiece, the only known work that was executed by both van Eyck and his brother Hubert. It expresses the main theme: the Lamb of God, simbolic of Christ's sacrifice. A Latin inscription on the altar reads, "Behold, the Lamb of God, which taketh away the sins of the world."*

XXXIII - JAN VAN EYCK: The Madonna with Chancellor Rolin - 1435 - Louvre, Paris - *This is considered one of van Eyck's most remarkable paintings. The central figures face each other in motionless poses so that time seems to stand still, and yet there is a sense of movement and liveliness in the bright background. It was this kind of accuracy of natural detail and intricacy of landscape that found such favor with the Italians.*

XXXIV-XXXV - HUGO VAN DER GOES: The Adoration of the Shepherds - c. 1476 - Uffizi Gallery, Florence - *This is the central panel of the famous Portinari Altarpiece, which had great influence on Florentine painters. The shepherds in this painting are particularly notable for the differentiated characterization of their features and expressions. Van der Goes employed the medieval practice of symbolic variance in size amongst the figures.*

XXXVI - HUGO VAN DER GOES: The Adoration of the Shepherds, detail from plates XXXIV and XXXV - *Van der Goes's ties with the traditions of Flemish realism are evident in this still life of the lily, columbine, and iris that symbolize the Passion of Christ and the sorrows of the Virgin.*

XXXVII - HUGO VAN DER GOES: The Temptation - Kunsthistorisches Museum, Vienna - *Van der Goes's powerful light and rounded figures are reminiscent of earlier Flemish masters like Campin, but the expressive intensity in the faces are particularly representative of the van der Goes style. This small panel painting, while influenced by the stage-setting and iconography of medieval mystery plays, displays the new sense of realism.*

XXXVIII - HUGO VAN DER GOES: Portrait of Maria Portinari and Her Daughter - c. 1476 - Uffizi Palace, Florence - *This is the right wing of the Portinari Altarpiece. Kneeling are the wife and one child of the donor and their patron saints. In the landscape, van der Goes has included some of his famous rustics.*

XXXIX - HUGO VAN DER GOES: Portrait of Maria Portinari and Her Daughter, detail from Plate XXXVIII - *Van der Goes was among the first to portray a child with proper child's proportions. He does the face and bodice masterfully, but the child's hands are much too large.*

XL - HUGO VAN DER GOES: Portrait of Tommaso Portinari and His Sons - c. 1476 - Uffizi Palace, Florence - *This is the left wing of the Portinari Altarpiece on which are portrayed the male members of the Portinari family, together with their patron Saint. It is interesting to note that Hans Memling also painted portraits of Tommaso and Maria Portinari. In the Memling portraits they have assumed the same positions and are wearing the same costumes.*

XLI - HUGO VAN DER GOES: Portrait of a Donor - Walters Art Gallery, Baltimore - *Van der Goes was greatly influenced by the work of van der Weyden, but instead of using that artist's aristocratic stylization in portraits, Van der Goes stressed a new gravity and solemnity. His deep religious spirituality and psychological insight brought a new emotional intensity to his portrayals of ordinary human beings.*

XLII-XLIII - HANS MEMLING: The Adoration of the Magi - c. 1480 - The Prado, Madrid - *Memling's inheritance from van der Weyden can be seen in striking fashion if this painting is compared to Plate XXII. The figures, their gestures, their costumes, the vessels that the kings offer are all so similar that it appears as if this work may have been some sort of tribute to the older painter.*

XLIV - HANS MEMLING: Virgin and Child - 1487 - Saint John's Hospital, Bruges - *This painting is the left wing of a diptych. Memling's widely acclaimed Madonnas all possessed a celestial sweetness, by which he creates a mystical feeling within the context of realism. His Madonnas were one of the major reasons for his international popularity.*

XLV - HANS MEMLING: The Crucifixion - Museo Civico, Vicenza - *This painting was commissioned by Jean Crabbe, a Cistercian abbot from the Abbey of the Dunes. Memling's ability to give his clients exactly what they wanted later brought him harsh criticism from critics who said he was too willing to adapt his style to their desires.*

XLVI - HANS MEMLING: The Crucifixion, detail from Plate XLV - *Memling tried to give equal importance to all the elements in his paintings. The fine colors and harmonies make this detail an excellent piece in its own right, and it shows that, if Memling did nothing to advance the art of Flemish realism, he did assimilate its basic ideals to a very high degree.*

XLVII - PIETER BRUEGEL: The Fight between Carnival and Lent, detail - 1559 - Kunsthistorisches Museum, Vienna - *Bruegel's earliest works are somewhat comic. On this occasion, he took advantage of Shrovetide to depict the Netherlandish peasant customs in detail. He shows both happy and somber sides of their life.*

XLVIII - PIETER BRUEGEL: The Dulle Griet (Mad Meg) - 1562 - Museum Mayer van den Bergh, Antwerp - *The central female figure of Mad Meg is the personification of the sin of covetousness. On the right, women are looting at the mouth of Hell. Above them, a tempter, with the face of a man and the clothes of a woman, tries to distract them by shoveling coins out of an egg.*

XLIX - PIETER BRUEGEL: The Fall of the Rebel Angels - 1562 - The Royal Museum of Fine Arts, Brussels - *This painting drew its inspiration from Bosch, whose paintings Bruegel had been encouraged to imitate when he was working for an engraver and print-seller. The Archangel Michael, together with his companions, fights against sins. The fallen angels are transformed into monsters.*

L-LI - PIETER BRUEGEL: Children's Games - 1560 - Kunsthistorisches Museum, Vienna - *The observation has been made that the children in this painting look more like adults than children. A great satirist, Bruegel shows the children as seriously absorbed in their games as adults are in their businesses. Seen from a higher perspective, the affairs of adults have as little significance as do the games of children.*

LII - PIETER BRUEGEL: The Triumph of Death - 1562 - The Prado, Madrid - *The army of the dead is fighting against the living. In the background is the barren landscape of Death. Here again we see the influence of Bosch and his conception of the Last Judgment.*

LIII - PIETER BRUEGEL: The Adoration of the Magi - 1564 - National Gallery, London - *This is one of the earliest of Bruegel's paintings to be influenced by Italian Renaissance art. The dominance of the large figures and the composition are Italian elements, but the individualization of the characters and the range of expressions are Flemish.*

LIV - PIETER BRUEGEL: The Return of the Herd - 1565 - Kunsthistorisches Museum, Vienna - *In 1565, Bruegel did a series of five paintings called the Months, which are considered by many to be among the greatest landscape paintings of the age. This painting, which is either October or November, was placed with the others in a frieze with a continuous background that connected one picture to the next.*

LV - PIETER BRUEGEL: The Hunters in the Snow - 1565 - Kunsthistorisches Museum, Vienna - *This is January from the series the Months. Bruegel's landscapes convey the idea that man is subordinate to nature. The simplicity of these landscapes is in sharp contrast to his more heavily detailed earlier paintings.*

LVI-LVII - PIETER BRUEGEL: The Procession to Calvary - 1564 - Kunsthistorisches Museum, Vienna - *This is Bruegel's largest painting. It also contains his most elaborate detailing. The theme of this painting is a condemnation of a hypocritical Christianity that outwardly displays piety without committing itself to the deeds that support holiness.*

LVIII - PIETER BRUEGEL: The Land of Cockaigne - 1567 - Alte Pinakothek, Munich - *The Dutch name Luilekkerland, for the fairytale land of Cockaigne, came from lui for lazy and lekker for gluttonous. This painting, with its immense amount of narrative detail, is a condemnation of the sin of gluttony.*

LIX - PIETER BRUEGEL: Peasant Wedding - 1567 - Kunsthistorisches Museum, Vienna - *Bruegel was famous for this type of anthropological painting in which he portrayed the peasants' everyday life of eating, drinking, and making merry. Bruegel's satire did not arise from snobbishness but from the fact that life in the lower classes was lived closer to the surface and therefore was more emblematic than the life of the bourgeoisie.*

LX-LXI - PIETER BRUEGEL: The Peasant Dance - 1567 - Kunsthistorisches Museum, Vienna - *Bruegel's strong feeling for folklore and earthiness is evident in the exuberance of the rustic common people. A religious celebration provides an occasion for the sinful behavior of lust, anger, and gluttony that Bruegel critically treats in this painting.*

LXII - PIETER BRUEGEL: The Gloomy Day, detail - 1565 - Kunsthistorisches Museum, Vienna - *This is February from the series the Months. Bruegel illustrates various facets of the month: the stormy sea in the landscape, the men busily pruning willows and tying twigs, and a child wearing a paper carnival crown and wrapped in pillows for warmth, holding the hand of a woman.*

LXIII - PIETER BRUEGEL: The Parable of the Blind - 1568 - National Museum, Naples - *This painting illustrates the parable from the Gospel of Saint Mathew: "If the blind lead the blind, both shall fall into the ditch." It is implied that the inner spiritual blindness is far worse then actual physical blindness, and Bruegel has managed to express the message in this late painting in a manner that is both harrowing and humorous.*

Hieronymus Bosch - The Adoration of The Magi

I

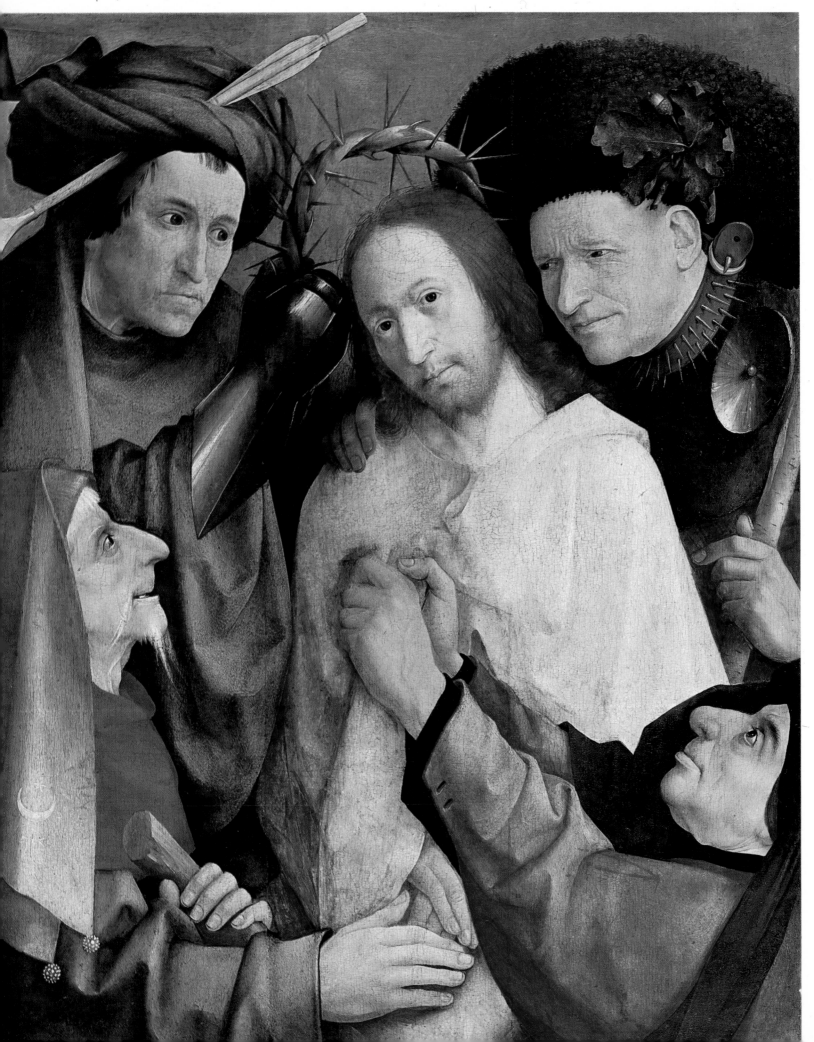

Hieronymus Bosch - Christ Bearing the Cross

Hieronymus Bosch - The Seven Deadly Sins and the Last Four Things

Hieronymus Bosch - The Prodigal Son

V

Hieronymus Bòsch - The Haywain

Hieronymus Bosch - The Haywain, detail of Plate VI

Hieronymus Bosch - The Temptation of St. Anthony, detail of Plate VIII

IX

Hieronymus Bosch - The Temptation of St. Anthony, detail

X

Hieronymus Bosch - St. Jerome Penitent

Hieronymus Bosch - St. John the Baptist in the Wilderness

XII

Hieronymus Bosch - The Garden of Delights, detail of Plate XIV

XVIII   *Petrus Christus - Portrait of Edward Grymestone*

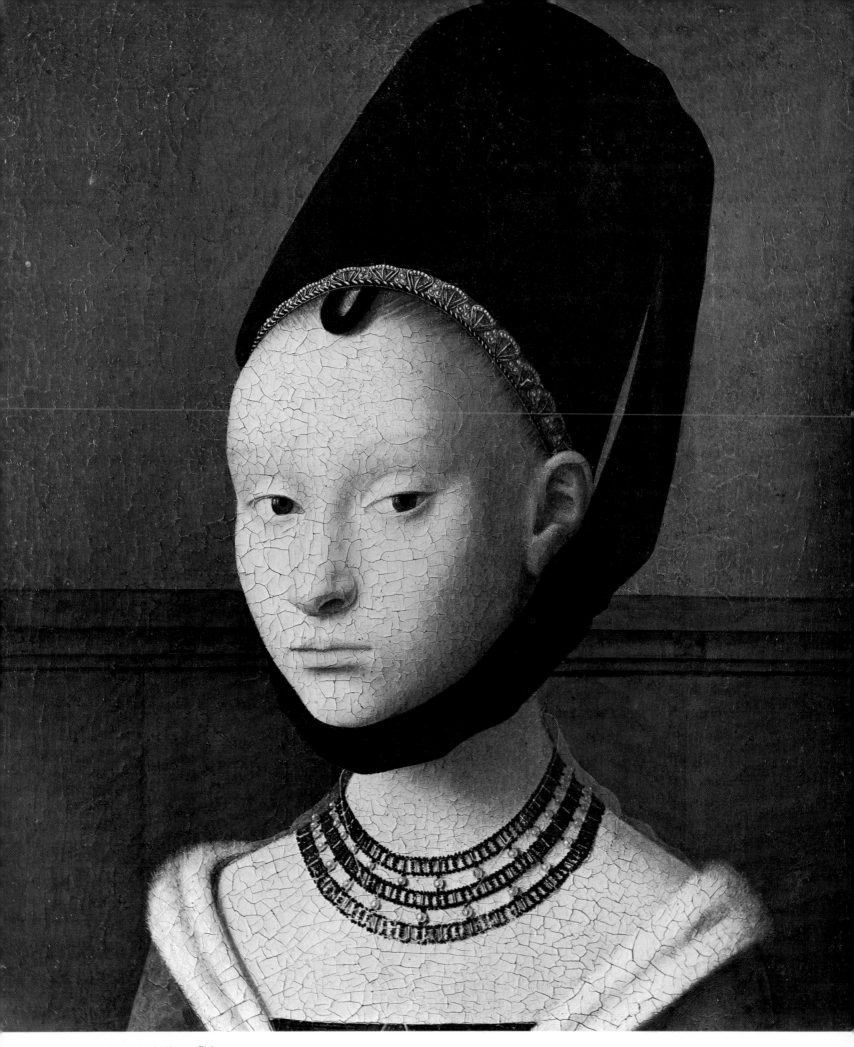

Petrus Christus - Portrait of a Young Girl

Rogier van der Weyden - The Adoration of the Magi

XXII

Rogier van der Weyden - The Adoration of the Magi, detail of Plate XXII

Rogier van der Weyden - Magdalene

Rogier van der Weyden - Portrait of a Lady

Rogier van der Weyden - The Annunciation

XXVIII

Jan van Eyck - The Arnolfini Wedding

Jan van Eyck - The Adoration of the Lamb

Jan van Eyck - The Madonna with Chancellor Rolin

Hugo van der Goes -
The Adoration of the Shepherds

Hugo van der Goes - The Original Sin

Hugo van der Goes - Portrait of Maria Portinari and Her Daughter

Hugo van der Goes - Detail from Plate XXXVIII

XL

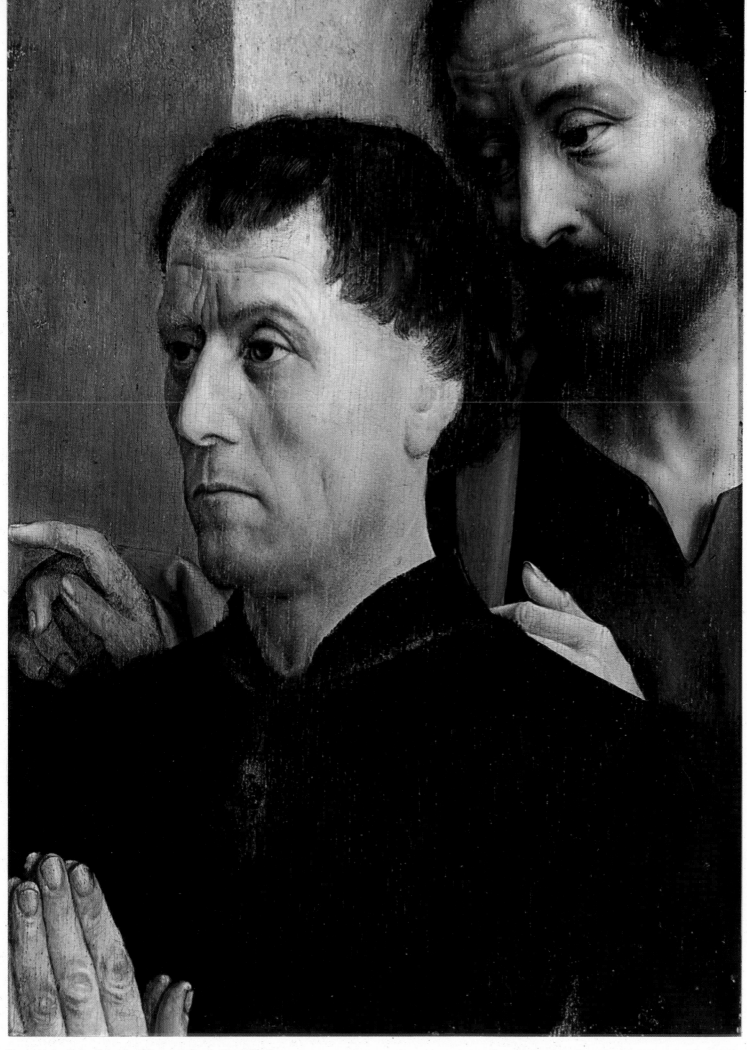

Hugo van der Goes - Portrait of Tommaso Portinari and His Sons

Hugo van der Goes - Portrait of donor with St. John Baptist

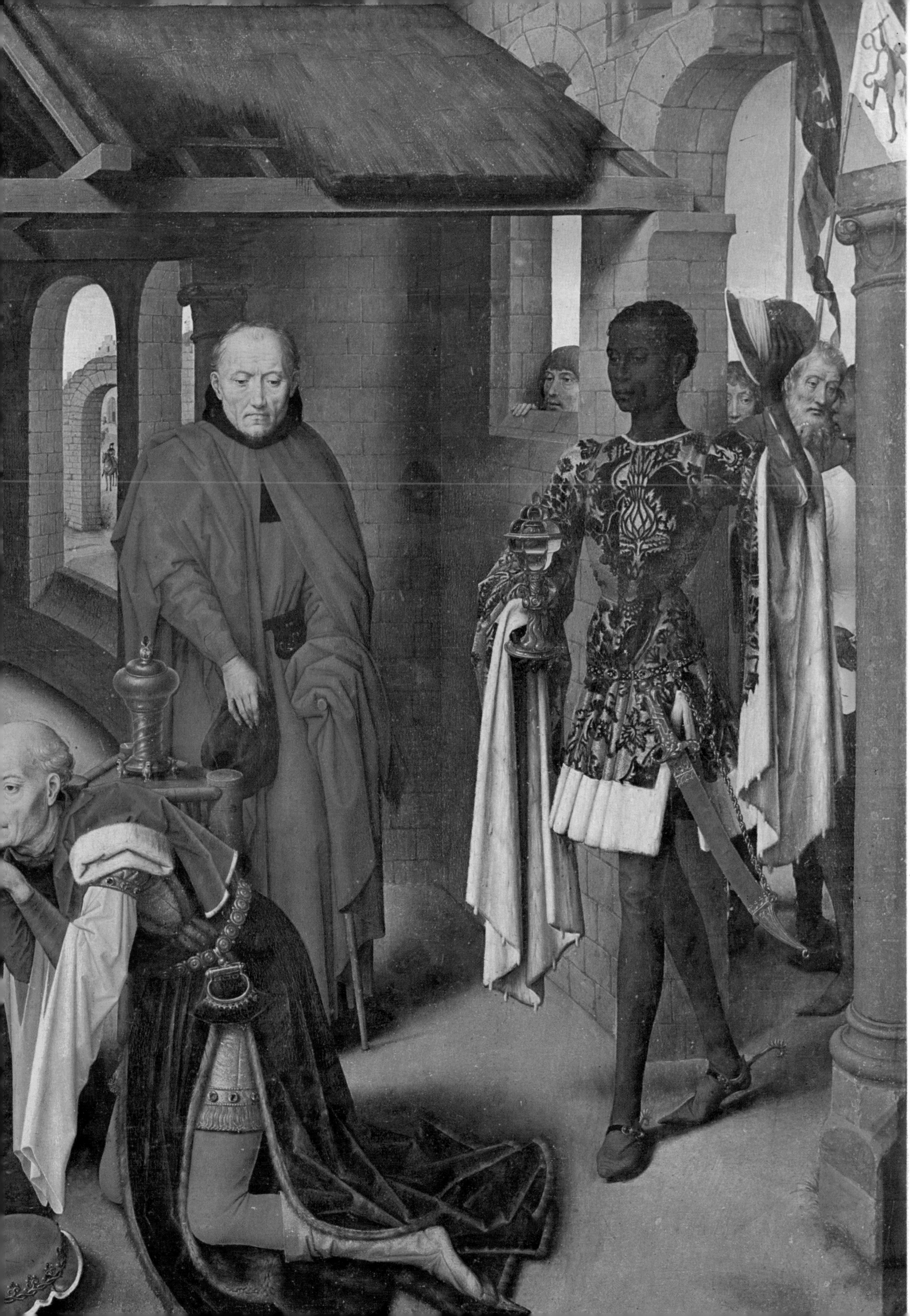

Hans Memling - The Adoration of the Magi

XLIII

Hans Memling - Virgin and Child

Hans Memling - The Crucifixion

Pieter Bruegel - The Fight between Carnival and Lent, detail

Pieter Bruegel - The Dulle Griet (Mad Meg)

Pieter Bruegel - The Fall of the Rebel Angels

Pieter Bruegel · Children's Games

Pieter Bruegel - The Triumph of Death

Pieter Bruegel - The Adoration of the Magi

Pieter Bruegel - The Return of the Herd

Pieter Bruegel - The Hunters in the Snow

Pieter Bruegel - The Procession to Calvary

Pieter Bruegel - The Land of Cockaigne

Pieter Bruegel - Peasant Wedding

Pieter Bruegel - The Peasant Dance

Pieter Bruegel - The Gloomy Day, detail

Pieter Bruegel - The Parable of the Blind

Illustrations from the Picture Archives of Fabbri Editori, Milan
Printed in January 1980, at the graphic plant of Fabbri Editori - Milan, Italy